Fold This Box

Single Sheet Designs for Origami Box Lovers

Volume 2

Bradley Tompkins

Paperback ISBN: 978-1-7361240-3-1

FoldThisBox.com

Contents

Names of these boxes are randomly drawn from my imagination (mostly streets in Northridge, California, a childhood memory, etc.).

Photo Index

Introduction

Welcome to this second volume of origami designs devoted to boxes and containers. Paper folding is more than a pastime for many origami enthusiasts. Whether you fold for enjoyment, challenge or curiosity, most people find the hobby a social craft. Share what you learn and fold with others and enjoy the many benefits that result from engaging the mind and hands in a hobby nearly anyone can master. Creative expression and the joy of learning brings lifelong benefits.

What makes origami special?

From minimal raw materials, a single sheet of paper becomes art in a matter of minutes!

Boxes and containers bring their own challenge and delight since every container has dimensions, volume, a base, walls and can hold something.

Maybe you love origami like I do, and that's why you are reading this book. Maybe it's learning new skills like paper crafts, or simply keeping your hands busy. Whatever your reason, by simply allowing your passion of learning new skills and designs, new pathways to creative expression emerge. That's what this book is about: learning new models to engage your mind and stimulate your thinking.

The end result? Tangible, handcrafted boxes you can use or give away. That's fun in itself, but if you "think outside the box", you'll see great intrinsic value in the learning process as well. Through repetition, you will build memory and communicate with others what you have learned.

How do you "build a better brain"? By continually learning new, challenging skills! Building new neural pathways through repetition, commitment and joyful involvement in a lifelong-practice yields benefits at any age.

Folding origami is fun and it's incredibly good for the mind. Learning new skills on a regular basis helps your mind remain young, vibrant and creative, regardless of your other hobbies, interests, or career path.

I hope you enjoy the book and will share your stories with me. Just search social media sites for @foldthisbox. Visit foldthisbox. com and see what others are learning and creating and join Origami USA if you're not already a member (origamiusa.org).

Some of the models shown in the photographs in this book show slight variations to accommodate the elephant hide paper used for the final images. Experiment for yourself and see what variations appeal to you and find videos on YouTube to explore some of these nuances.

This book contains a small selection of hundreds of boxes I have designed over the years. The index number that appears (261) in a circle on diagrams references the master list of designs, just for ease of searching and sorting. Looking for more boxes to fold? Watch for future volumes in this series!

Happy folding!

First Things First

Have you ever stared at assembly instructions from a product or package and wondered how something could look so complicated? When first starting out on any pursuit, it's very easy to run up against terms and definitions, illustrations and instructions that are hard to understand. My goal in writing this book centers on making the results achievable and the concepts clear! I have been there too, staring at instructions with no one to guide me. Sometimes the diagrams aren't consistent with other authors. Sometimes the language is foreign. Let's get on some common ground to start.

Everyone who writes a book on origami has the challenge of presenting those first steps for beginners. Basic diagrams of preliminary folds, bases and terms for origami are the same all around the world. How we communicate them is not the same. Have a look at a handful of origami books (as I have in preparing this text), and you'll see some commonalities, and some big differences! There are some terrific books for beginners, showing very clear photos of folds. I encourage you to obtain several and read through them, trying the basics until you have mastered them. The best way to learn might be to get an experienced folder to demonstrate while reading a diagram. You simply must understand the "rules" for folding before trying complicated models. That way you have a better chance when you attempt an advanced model.

Following are the key terms and techniques you need when folding models presented in this book.

Valley Crease

Take a sheet of paper and fold one side to the opposite side, matching the edges. If you carefully hold the edges together so they don't slip, then crease the paper along the center, you'll have a valley fold. Open the paper and observe! It looks like a valley, where water might follow along.

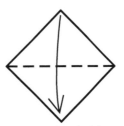

A mountain fold is just the opposite. A mountain fold is just a valley fold, viewed from the other side of the paper! The diagram will show a dashed line with dots, as shown below.

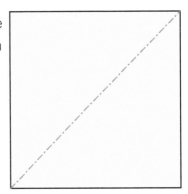

This book does not employ other origami combinations like, squash folds, inside reverse, outside reverse or any of the traditional "bases" (frog base, fish base, waterbomb base, etc.), so I'll leave you to discover and use those models to create the many wonderful basic and advanced creations in traditional origami.

Crease

After making a fold, if it is "unfolded", you are left with a crease. You cannot "uncrease". You can only unfold.

Fold

A fold results from creasing to a given point and leaving it in place.

Precreases

Precreasing can be an enjoyable part of folding and it provides visual landmarks for steps that follow. Precreasing can take a long time in folding tessellations, because the entire sheet is usually creased into many sub-divisions.

In this book, when you see a set of creases in the diagram, and you don't see those creases on your own paper, your job is to get those creases on your sheet before moving on! "Reading" the diagram means that you look again after a few creases and compare your model to the diagram. In general, when you see a solid line in a diagram, that indicates a completed crease from a previous step. Solid lines indicate that the creases exist but are not used in the current step.

The sheet has been creased into thirds, and the next step is to crease the edges to the "one-third" landmark.

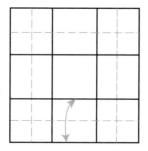

Uneven Division

You probably know how to fold a sheet in half, but how about "thirds or fifths"?

In this book, when you see a set of precreases in uneven division, such as thirds, you need to apply a technique to divide the sheet into thirds or fifths. We know how to divide a sheet in two: simply fold one edge to the other and crease! Presto: two halves, of equal size. For division by thirds or fifths, you need another method. When you see "Crease (or mark) in thirds" you need

The Fujimoto Method of Uneven Division

This technique provides a quick, fairly accurate way to get a sheet into thirds or fifths. Fold the right side to a point on the left where you "see" equal distance from the left side to the temporary edge location. You're estimating here, so don't crease! Instead, "mark" the right side by very gently pressing down just along the top.

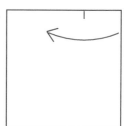

That's your first landmark. Fold the left side to that mark and gently mark the left side.

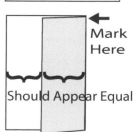

Open the paper and you'll see your two tick marks at the top.

How accurate were your estimates? To find out, fold the right edge to the left tick mark. If you're accurate, the right tick mark will fall naturally on the spot you've just creased.

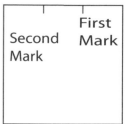

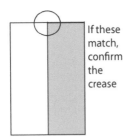

If these match, confirm the crease

If it's a little off, split the difference and go ahead and crease down the entire length of the paper. Do the same on the left side. Try this technique several times on fresh sheets of paper and you'll soon develop a knack for finding the exact thirds of a sheet of paper in no time.

Divide in 5ths

For fifths, you follow a similar procedure, but you form preliminary estimates based on what looks like one third of the page width.

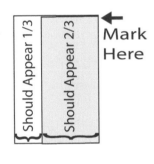

Should Appear 1/3   Should Appear 2/3   **Mark Here**

Make a light mark on the right side, open, then create another mark by creasing the right edge to the first mark.

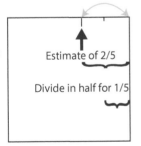

Estimate of 2/5

Divide in half for 1/5

Continue marking by folding the left edge over to the 2nd mark, then dividing it in half. Again, if you practice this several times, you'll quickly

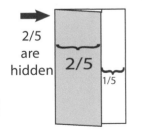

2/5 are hidden   2/5   1/5

develop the ability to divide a sheet into fifths. It's actually more complicated to explain than to do it.

Valley crease the inner 1/5"

Follow the Fujimoto method shown above, but only crease the inner 1/5. The preliminary marks will leave a center 1/5 in the middle of the page.

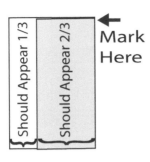

Should Appear 1/3   Should Appear 2/3   **Mark Here**

Isolated Creases

When you see a small crease out in the middle of a diagram, you have to make that crease without creasing across the entire sheet. To

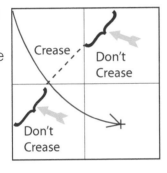

Crease   Don't Crease   Don't Crease

crease just a small portion, flip the edge to the point indicated and crease with your fingernail or bone folder just along the part to be creased. I refer to this as "preserving" the segment. Why go to this extra effort? The answer lies in "My Rules for Origami Boxes": to avoid preliminary creases that are not part of the structure of the box, isolated creases are required. The resulting model displays only smooth, uncreased planes. A personal prefererence eventually became a habit, then a rule.

"Mark 1/2 and outer quarters"

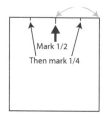

This instruction indicates you are to mark the center along the top edge (and bottom edge if you like). Simply fold one edge to the other, and mark. Open back up and fold the right edge to the first mark, mark again. Repeat on the left side. Open back up and you should see three tick marks. These landmarks are to be used in the completing the model.

"Crease Inner 1/4"

This instruction indicates the basis of the model is 1/8s. Mark 1/2 and 1/4, then fold one edge to the opposite 1/4. Repeat on the opposite side. This will put 1/4 of the paper in the center with 3/8 on either side.

"The colored side down"

Most inexpensive origami paper is one-sided: a color or design on one on the "good" side, and white on the other. More expensive origami paper is two-sided, with a color or pattern on one side, and another on the opposite side. When the diagram says "colored side down" that means you must pick the colored side on one-sided paper, and begin folding with that colored side down against the paper. Most diagrams indicate the colored portion of a model by shading, and leaving everything else blank or white.

"Model becomes 3D" or 3D

This is the point that when you collapse or raise a wall, the model will no longer lay flat on the table. The diagram will also look different, because all steps from that point forward indicate a 3-dimensional object, not a flat one. You will likely be folding "in the air" from that point forward.

Pleat Fold

If you are shown a mountain fold along side a valley fold, the arrows will indicate the direction. Grab the mountain by pinching it and fold it to the point indicated. The paper is now several layers thick.

Crease a Rim

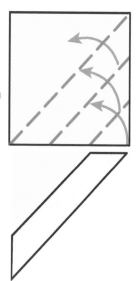

This direction indicates that you are to fold the edge to a landmark, then roll the two layers again to another point. This will form a rim in which the original raw edge is completely concealed, similar to a hem in a garment.

Mark the Center 1/2

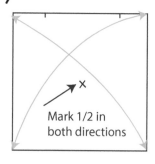

Crease one corner to the opposite corner and "mark" gently. Open and crease the other diagonal to the opposite corner andside and mark. This will leave a "+" or "X" where the two marks intersect.

My Rules for Origami Boxes

1. Hide raw edges. When possible, the raw edge is tucked, hidden or lies adjacent to other edges so they are not easily visible.

2. No "leftover" creases. Whenever possible, avoid preliminary creases that are visible on the finished model in open flat planes of a finished model (with the exception of collapsible boxes which have crease lines to allow the collapse).

3. Sturdy. Some locking mechanism or use of surface tension prevent the box from flopping open.

Collapse the Model
Many models in this volume feature a somewhat challenging step: "Collapse along existing crease lines." This means the model will get much smaller because multiple layers will be stacked.

Tips for success:
Ensure that all valley and mountain creases are confirmed. Go over each one and make sure they are neat and not pinched or reversed.

Work around the model several times, nudging the paper toward the center. This will reveal kinks or missed pre-creases. When the pre-creases are correct, the model will usually collapse with very light touch.

Use a "bone folder". They don't make them out of bone anymore but find something that you like. Here is mine: a wooden instrument for crafting clay, purchased at an art store.

Steps in a Collapse

Finding an anchor point to push toward center.

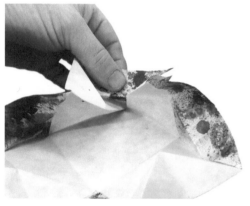

Pushing down toward the table. Let the paper spring back and move to the other corners.

This symbol indicates a difficult step in this book.

Mountains and valley creases confirmed.

Partial collapse.

Closer to flattened.

Resolve any resistant creases.

Completed and ready for final pressing with bone folder.

Single - Sheet Origami Boxes

Many satisfying boxes can be fold from blintzing corners to the center. The traditional Masu box provides inspiration many boxes: every box feature some allotment of the initial surface for a base (the portion which remains flat on the surface) and the rest of the paper for walls and rims. Boxes generally fall into one of three categories: open, closable and collapsible. The following pages provide a wide range of experiences in folding, both in terms of the sequential steps described and the final product. Origami is as much about the process as the completed model. Happy folding!

Open Box   Closable   Collapsible

Cavit Box

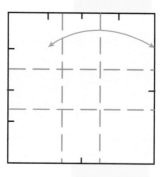

On color-side UP, crease inner 1/4. (Mark 1/2 and 1/4; crease edge to opposite 1/4 mark.) Crease lightly through center, as it will be reversed.

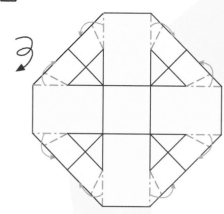

Turn over and pleat mountain creases to adjacent sides. Model will become 3D with each side completed.

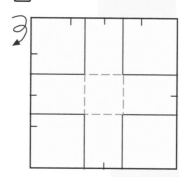

Turn over and reverse base from mountain to valley creases.

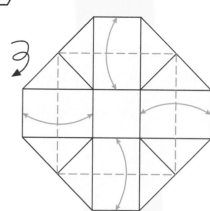

Turn over and valley crease sides to center base.

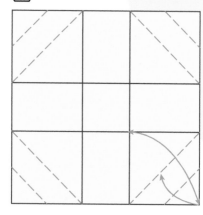

Crease corners to the intersection. Halve then flop to form a rim.

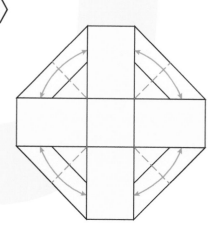

Crease diagonals. Do not crease through center base.

14

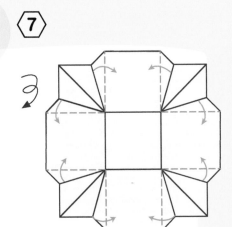

⟨7⟩

Turn model over and confirm triangular flaps fall toward center panels.

Bottom view shown.

⟨8⟩

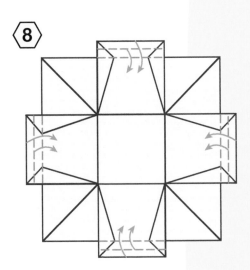

Fold outer rim in half and flop in place, forming locks.

⟨9⟩

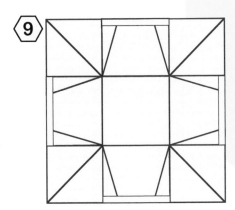

CSI Box

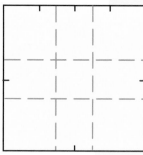

On color side down, crease inner 1/4. (Mark 1/2 and 1/4; crease edge to opposite 1/4 mark.)

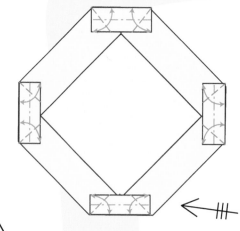

Crease corners of each rectangle in at 45 degree angle. Two layers are creased.

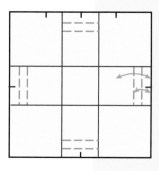

Valley crease at 1/4 and 1/8 mark in center panels.

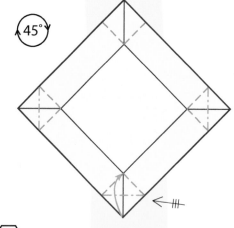

Open corners flat.

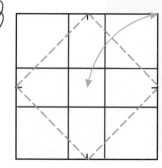

Turn over and crease corners to center.

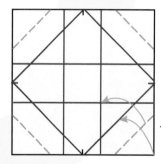

Fold corner to diagonal, then flop along diagonal.

114

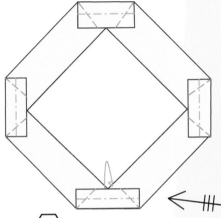

Drop raw edge of each rectangle behind, concealing them.

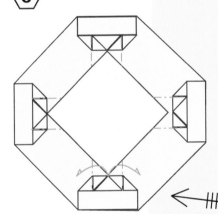

Mountain fold triangular structures behind (two layers).

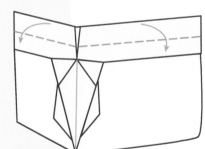

Halve the rim, dropping to 90 degrees as shown in photo.

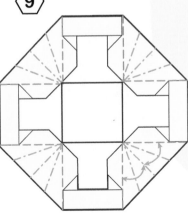

Confirm valley creases match underlying creases, then mountain crease center of each segment in half, then align with adjacent valley crease to halve, forming kite shape.

Raise to 3D, then tuck triangular tabs into underlying slot on either side. Outside view of one corner shown.

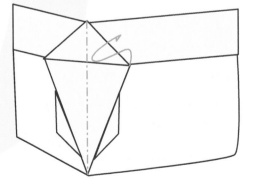

Tampa Box

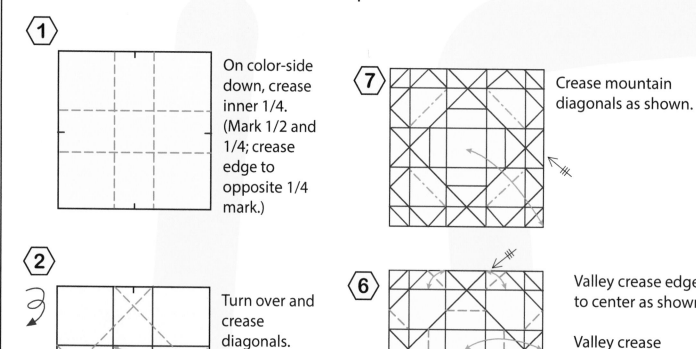

1 On color-side down, crease inner 1/4. (Mark 1/2 and 1/4; crease edge to opposite 1/4 mark.)

7 Crease mountain diagonals as shown.

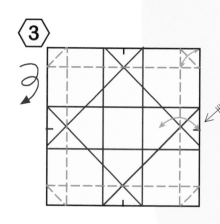

2 Turn over and crease diagonals.

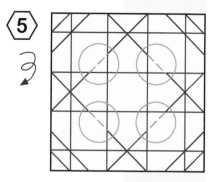

6 Valley crease edges to center as shown.

Valley crease diagonals as shown.

3 Crease corners on 1/8 diagonals. Then valley crease along 1/8 outer perimiters.

5 Reverse mountain to valley in inner diagonals as shown.

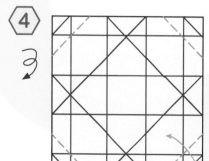

4 Turn over and valley crease diagonals along intersections made in previous step.

279

18

8 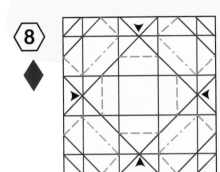 Collapse model along existing creases.

 9 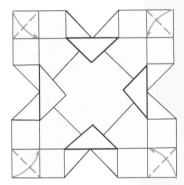 Fold corners in.

14 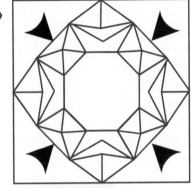 Turn model over and depress on triangular shapes to complete bottom of the box.

 10 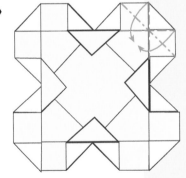 Collapse corners.

13 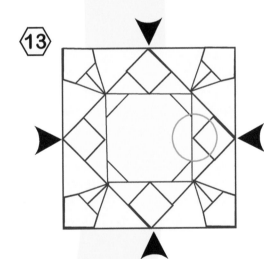 Hold center rim where shown and and expand box by depressing underlying structure along existing crease lines.

11 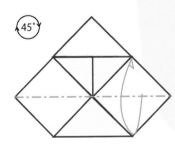 Rotate 45 degrees and flop triangular flaps under. One corner shown.

Repeat on other three corners.

12 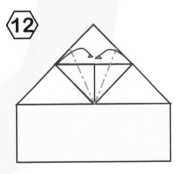 Mountain crease flap edges to center point, concealing raw edges. Repeat on other three corners.

Canoga Box

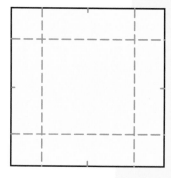

Color side down, mark fifths then valley crease outer 1/5 on all four sides.

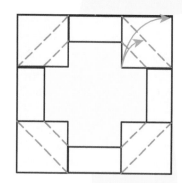

Rim fold corners diagonally.

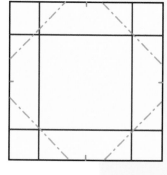

Mountain Crease diagonals through corner intersections..

Mountain crease inner segments to inner base.

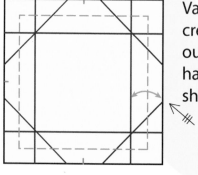

Valley crease outer 1/5 in half as shown.

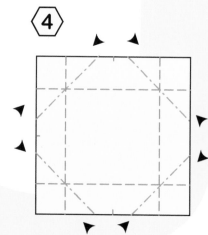

Collapse model using existing creases.

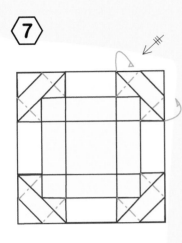

⑦ Mountain crease each corner segment behind, concealing.

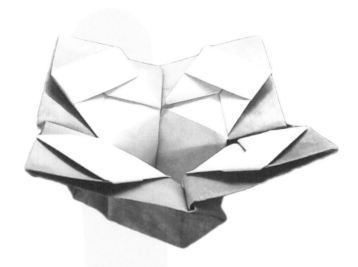

⑧ Crease corners to opposite intersection. Crease both ways and confirm orientations as shown.

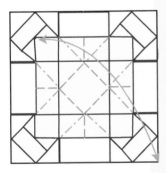

⑪

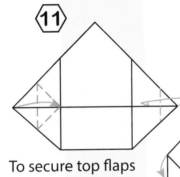

To secure top flaps in a flat position, on the outside, fold point in and crease sharply backward.

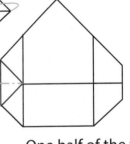

One half of the triangle structure should lie parallel with the rim flap.

⑨ Form 3D by bringing points together. Repeat for the other sides.

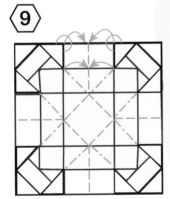

⑩

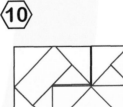
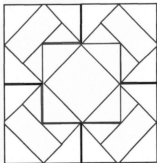

Superior Box

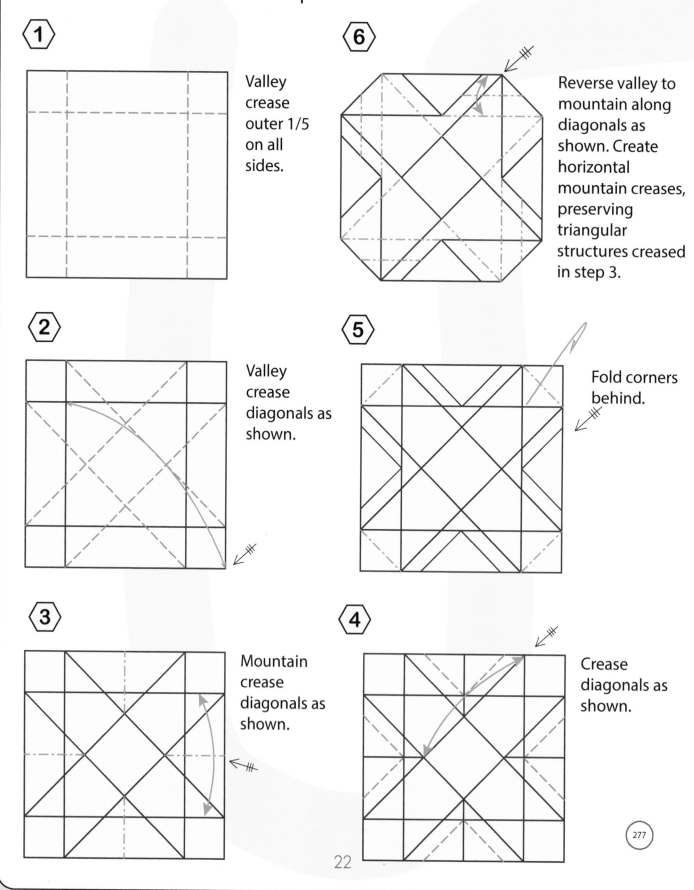

1 Valley crease outer 1/5 on all sides.

2 Valley crease diagonals as shown.

3 Mountain crease diagonals as shown.

4 Crease diagonals as shown.

5 Fold corners behind.

6 Reverse valley to mountain along diagonals as shown. Create horizontal mountain creases, preserving triangular structures creased in step 3.

⑦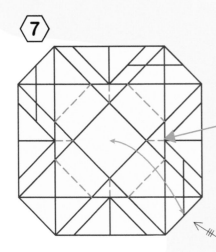

Valley crease wall height as shown.

Reverse horizontal and vertical creases (inside the tiny triangles) from mountain to valley.

⑧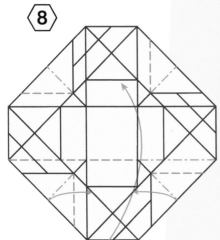

Raise one side of the box along existing crease lines at center base. Mountain diagonals will drop behind as you hold the partially 3D model shown in next step.

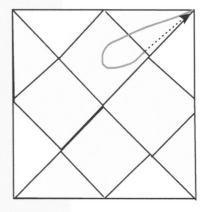

After interlacing flaps, tuck each corner behind underlying flap.

⑪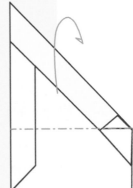

Drop flap onto top of box and repeat steps 8 -10 for the remaining sides. Rotate to the left from this step.

⑨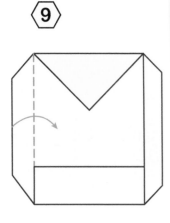

One side shown. Fold left segment to the right along existing crease line. Partial 3D.

⑩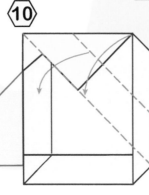

Fold segments down from the top right to the bottom left along existing crease lines.

Omaha Box

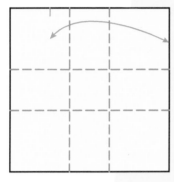

Color side down, crease inner 1/4 (Mark 1/2 and 1/4; crease edge to opposite 1/4 mark.

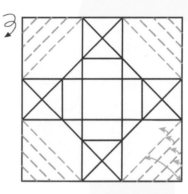

Turn over and crease corners to diagonal; open, halve again and rim fold past original diagonal

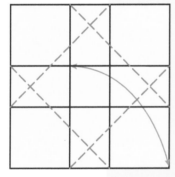

Crease corners to opposite intersections.

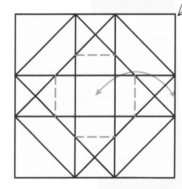

Valley crease edges to center along inner segment only.

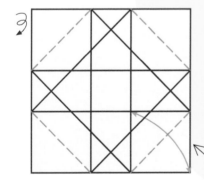

Turn over and valley crease corners to inner base.

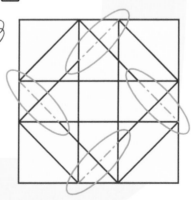

Turn over and reverse valley to mountain along diagonals shown.

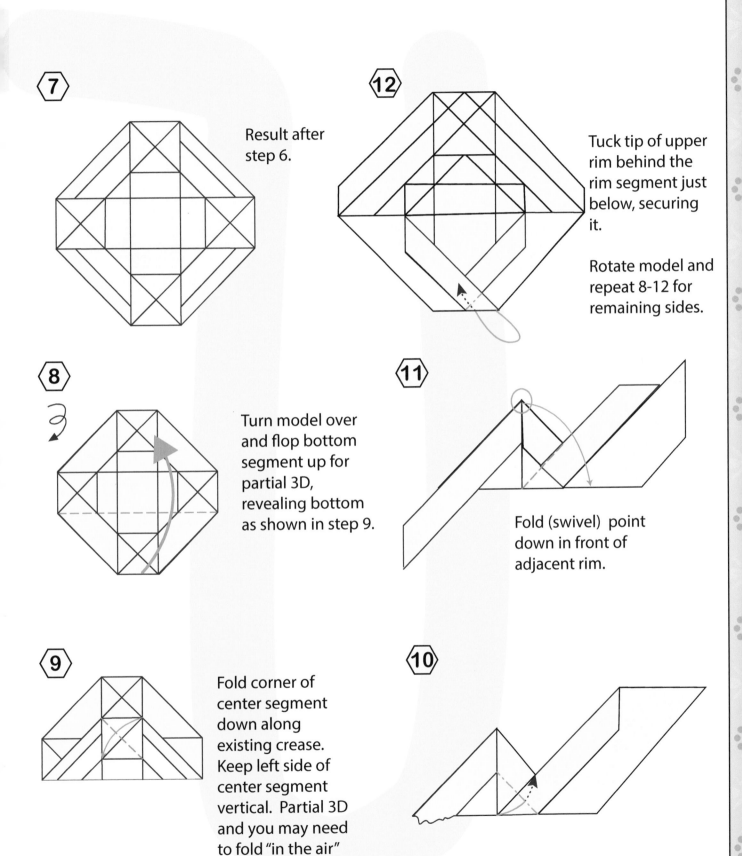

⑦

Result after step 6.

⑫

Tuck tip of upper rim behind the rim segment just below, securing it.

Rotate model and repeat 8-12 for remaining sides.

⑧

Turn model over and flop bottom segment up for partial 3D, revealing bottom as shown in step 9.

⑪

Fold (swivel) point down in front of adjacent rim.

⑨

Fold corner of center segment down along existing crease. Keep left side of center segment vertical. Partial 3D and you may need to fold "in the air" for remaining

⑩

(13)

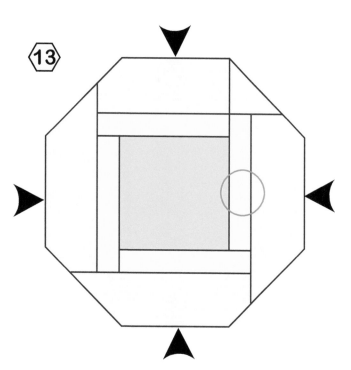

Hold rim firmly where shown and raise box walls by depressing the diamond shapes on the outside of the box. Resecure flap tips as necessary after expanding box.

(14)

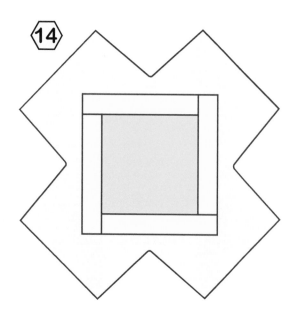

Dutch Box

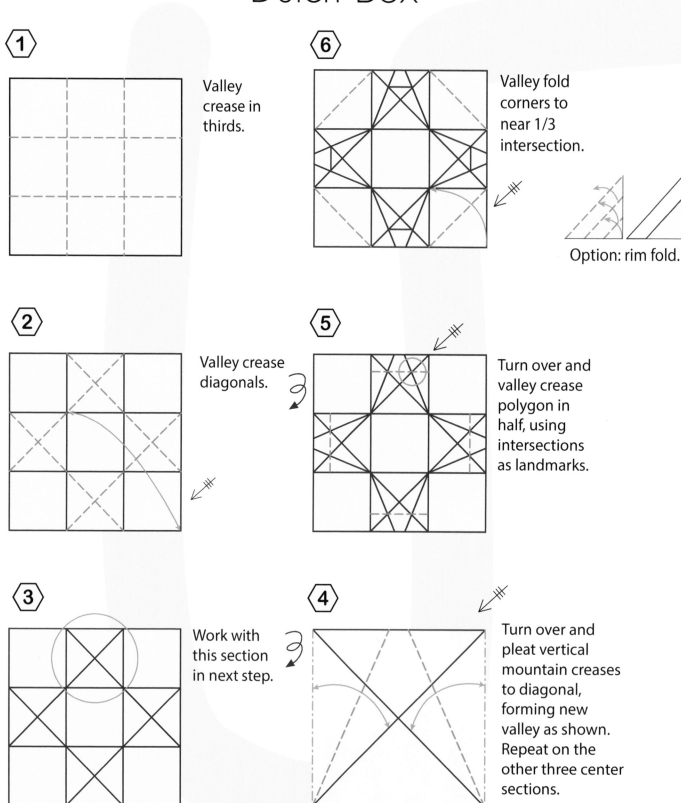

1. Valley crease in thirds.

2. Valley crease diagonals.

3. Work with this section in next step.

4. Turn over and pleat vertical mountain creases to diagonal, forming new valley as shown. Repeat on the other three center sections.

5. Turn over and valley crease polygon in half, using intersections as landmarks.

6. Valley fold corners to near 1/3 intersection.

Option: rim fold.

72

⟨7⟩

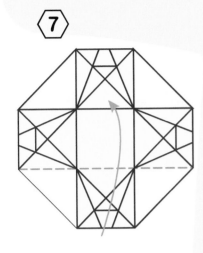

Flop bottom up to complete next step.

⟨8⟩

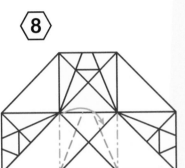

Pleat mountain on left to diagonal.

Partially 3D for remaining steps.

⟨11⟩

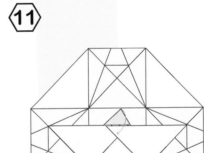

Fold triangular structure behind outer wall, concealing. Rotate model to the left and repeat steps 7-11.

⟨9⟩

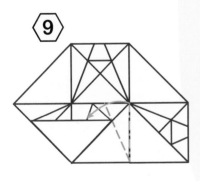

Pleat mountain on the right side over the left triangle from previous step.

⟨10⟩

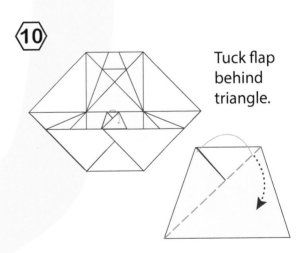

Tuck flap behind triangle.

Acute Box

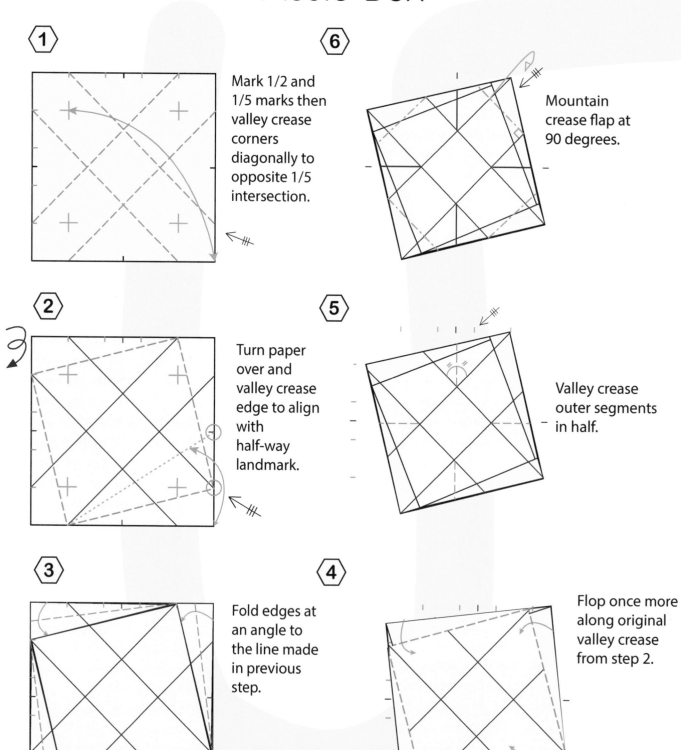

1

Mark 1/2 and 1/5 marks then valley crease corners diagonally to opposite 1/5 intersection.

2

Turn paper over and valley crease edge to align with half-way landmark.

3

Fold edges at an angle to the line made in previous step.

4

Flop once more along original valley crease from step 2.

5

Valley crease outer segments in half.

6

Mountain crease flap at 90 degrees.

30

7

7

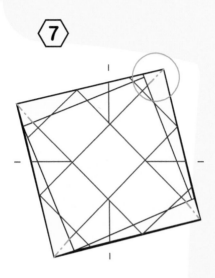

Confirm mountain crease of rim aligns with underlying mountain crease. Depending on paper thickness, this flap may be tucked behind.

8

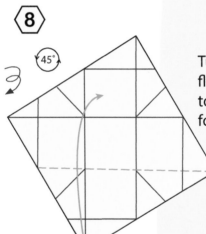

45°

Turn model over and flop triangular flaps toward center panels for the next step.

11

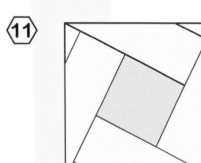

Interlace flaps.

9

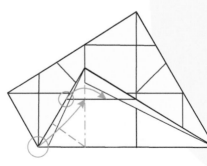

Pleat from left to right, forming partial 3D. The valley crease goes behind the raised structure.

10

Drop rim back to top of box.

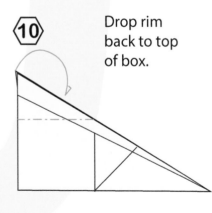

Rotate model to the left and repeat steps 8 and 9 for the remaining sides.

Snapdragon Box

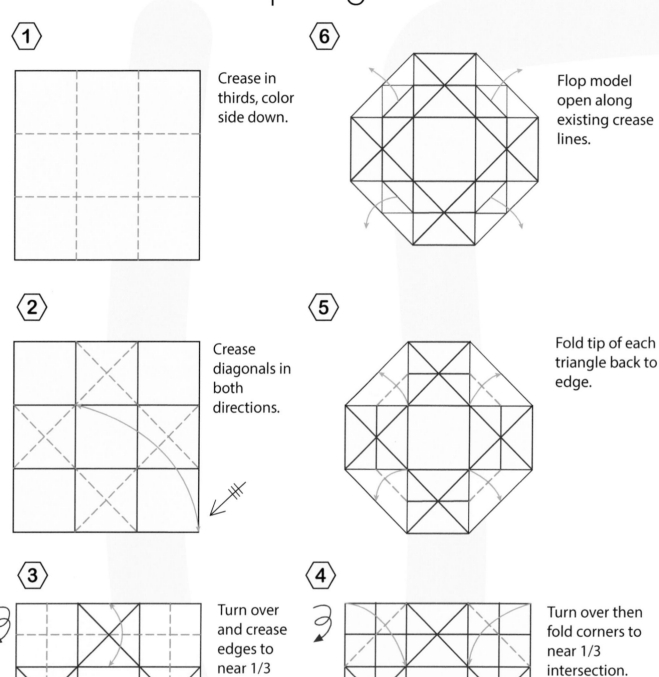

1 Crease in thirds, color side down.

2 Crease diagonals in both directions.

3 Turn over and crease edges to near 1/3 landmarks.

4 Turn over then fold corners to near 1/3 intersection.

5 Fold tip of each triangle back to edge.

6 Flop model open along existing crease lines.

14

⬧ (7)

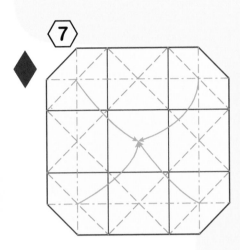

Confirm
mountain and
valley creases
and collapse.
Work each corner
separately

(8)

(1/4)

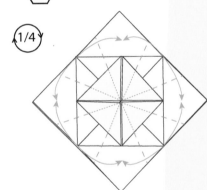

Fold underlying
structure in half,
securing against
the diagonal walls.
This forms a kite
shape on each
corner and conceals
all raw edges.

(9)

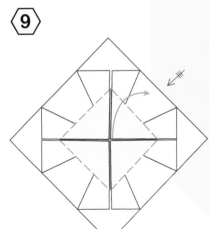

Fold center
triangles back.
They will tend to
stay upright in
the final
treatment.

(10)

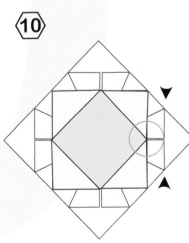

Grasp upper
structure with
thumb and
forefinger where
shown and
squeeze
underlying base to
expand the box.
Repeat for each
corner. Shape final
box as desired.

Allie Box

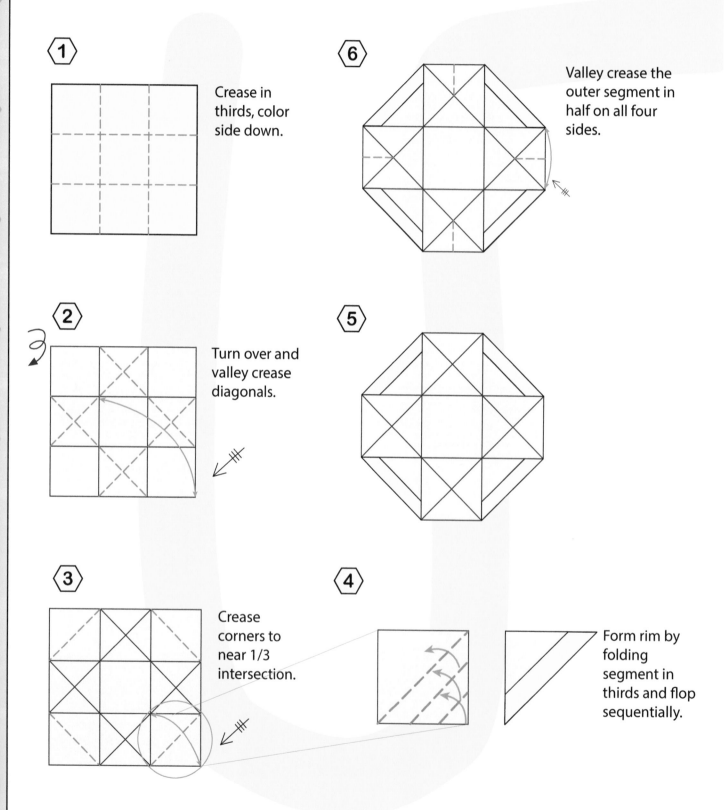

1 Crease in thirds, color side down.

2 Turn over and valley crease diagonals.

3 Crease corners to near 1/3 intersection.

4 Form rim by folding segment in thirds and flop sequentially.

5

6 Valley crease the outer segment in half on all four sides.

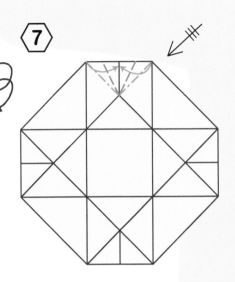

(7) Pleat mountain diagonals to center. Model becomes 3D at this point. Hold firmly and turn over for next step.

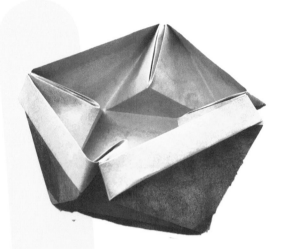

(8) Form a corner lock by folding tips down across horizontal edge. If you fold a little lower than the paper edge, you will avoid a raw edge shown in step 9. Squeeze the triangles together to secure.

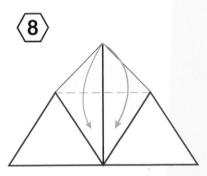

Rotate and repeat step 7 and 8 for the remaining corners.

(9) Depending on the paper used, you may find a segment with a raw edge protruding along the lower line of the rim. Tuck this under the rim for a stronger finished box.

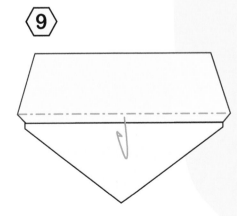

Camel Box

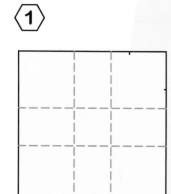

1 On color side down, crease inner 1/4. (Mark 1/2 and 1/4; crease edge to opposite 1/4 mark.)

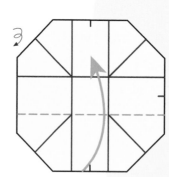

6 Turn over and flop bottom 3/8 up along existing crease line for next step.

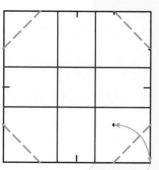

2 Crease corners to outer 1/4 mark, then halve the segment and form a rim.

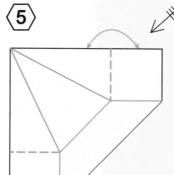

5 Valley crease horizontal and vertical segment as shown on each corner panel.

3

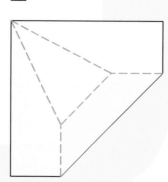

4 Valley crease layer below to match rim segment.

Form valley crease between corner and rim as shown.

31

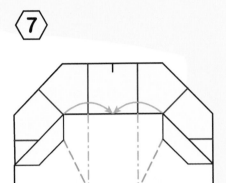

⑦

Pleat adjacent points behind to center of middle wall panel. Model becomes 3D from this step forward.

⑧

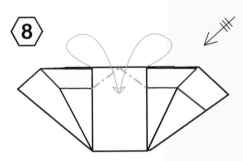

Fold corners behind (two layers), securing. Rotate and repeat for all sides.

Tip: depending on paper thickness, you may find it easier to perform steps 7 and 8 together.

Elephant hide, used for models on most photos in this book, may be tinted with India ink for a very sturdy box with two colors!

⑨

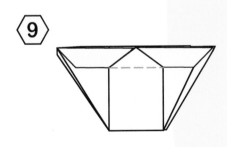

Shape final box rim by carefully valley creasing through all layers. Do not bend top surface of rim.

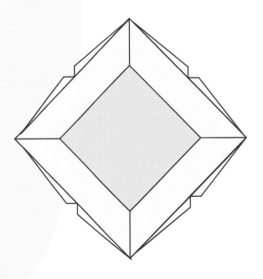

Yanagi Box

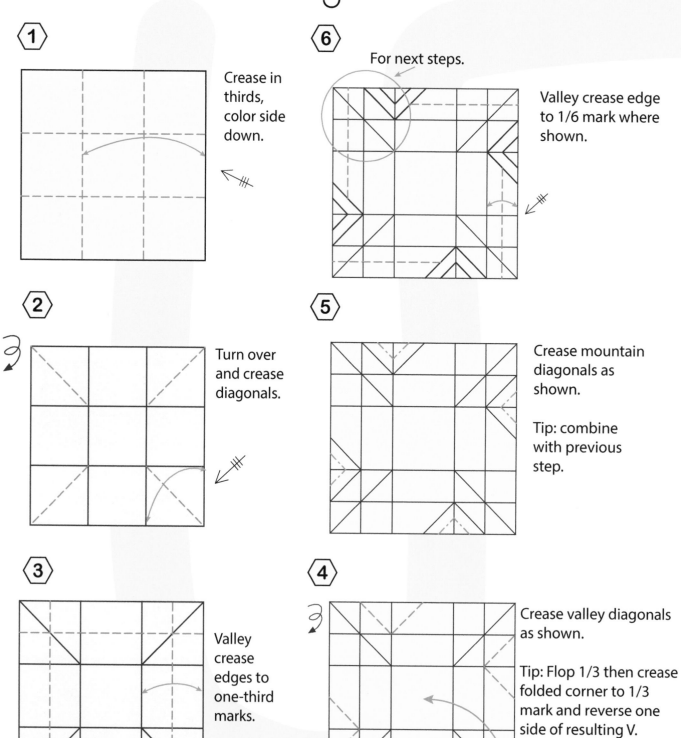

1 Crease in thirds, color side down.

2 Turn over and crease diagonals.

3 Valley crease edges to one-third marks.

4 Crease valley diagonals as shown.

Tip: Flop 1/3 then crease folded corner to 1/3 mark and reverse one side of resulting V.

5 Crease mountain diagonals as shown.

Tip: combine with previous step.

6 For next steps.

Valley crease edge to 1/6 mark where shown.

89

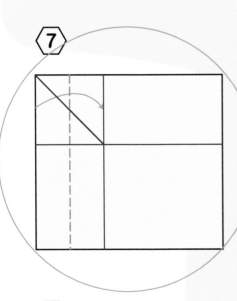

7

Fold left segment to the right.

Upper left corner shown for steps 7-10.

8

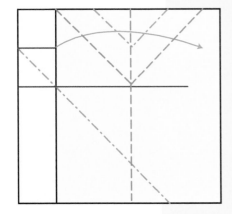

Flop along 1/3 valley crease for partial 3D.

11

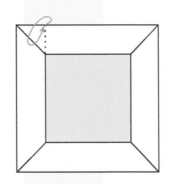

Tuck flap into pocket on all four corners.

9

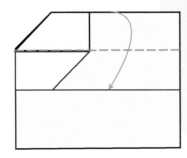

Fold top segment down.

10

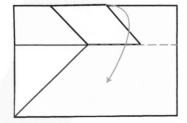

Fold down again, concealing corner.

Repeat 7-10 for remaining corners.

Sequal Box

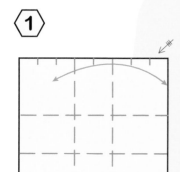

① 1 On color side down, crease inner 1/4. (Mark 1/2 and 1/4; crease edge to opposite 1/4 mark.)

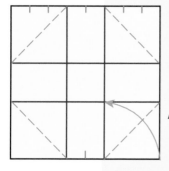

② 2 Fold corners to near intersection.

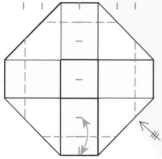

③ 3 Crease edges to 1/4 point on all four sides.

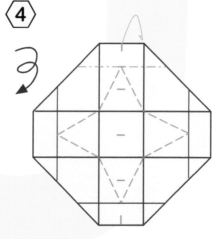

④ 4 Turn model over and crease diagonals as shown. You may find it easiest to drop the segment back from previous step.

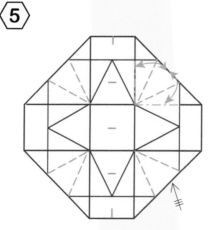

⑤ 5 Pleat new valley creases by aligning existing mountain creases to center of outer diagonals

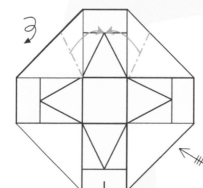

⑥ 6 Turn over and bring diagonals formed in step 5 toward the center and press firmly. Repeat with each wall segment.

Model becomes 3D.

110

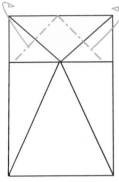

Mountain crease corners behind.

Inside view of one side shown.

⟨8⟩

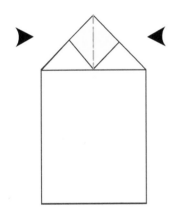

Squeeze points together to form a single triangular segment.

⟨9⟩

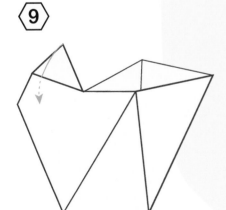

Insert this segment by tucking it into the pocket on either side.

Repeat steps 7-9 for remaining sides.

⟨10⟩

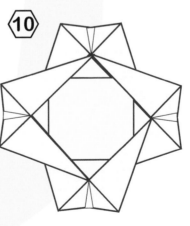

Then flatten the segments back out, completing the box. (Top view).

Ventura Box

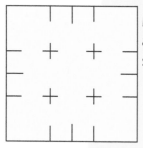

Mark 1/2 and 1/3 as shown.

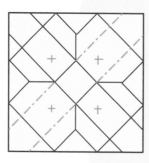

Reverse these valley creases to mountain. Note orientation for remaining steps.

②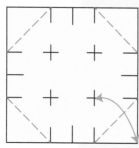

Crease corners to near 1/3 intersection.

⑤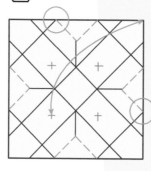

Crease valley diagonals: each corner to opposite 1/3 landmark. Rotate left and repeat 3x.

③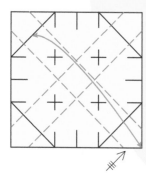

The sheet is divided into 9 equal squares. Crease corners to center of square on the opposite side, forming a long diagonal. Rotate and repeat for four diagonals as shown.

④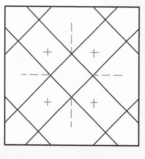

Crease from center square on each side as shown.

42

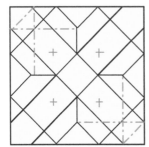

Add these mountain creases.

Rotate model 45 degrees and Raise to 3D along existing creases. A pair of tongue and groove structures will be formed next.

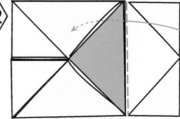

Top view. Insert tab segments into slots to close the box. Left tab shown complete.

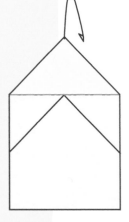

Fold groove flap 90 degrees back to top of box. Repeat on opposite side.

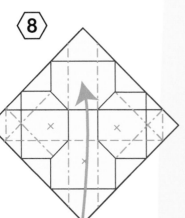

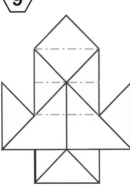

Tongue: fold top corner behind, followed by the next segment. Fold the last mountain crease just 90 degrees, as this forms the top of the box. Repeat on opposite side.

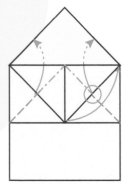

Rotate model to show groove side. Open the slit from left to right along underlying valley crease. Hide small flap under top triangular structure.

Arcadia Box

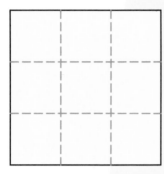

Color side down, crease in thirds.

⑥

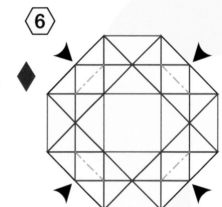

Using mountain crease as an anchor, work each side to collapse box along existing creases.

②

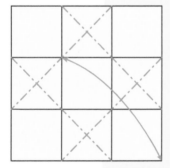

Mountain crease diagonals.

⑤

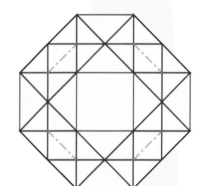

Mountain crease through both layers. Or open and perform creases separately.

③

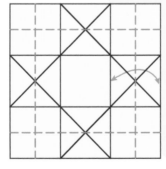

Crease edges to near 1/3 intersection on all four sides.

④

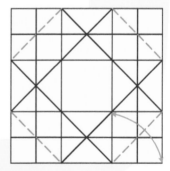

Crease all four corners to near 1/3 intersections.

(269)

44

⟨7⟩

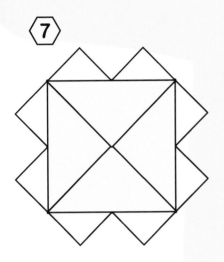

After collapse in step 6.

⟨8⟩

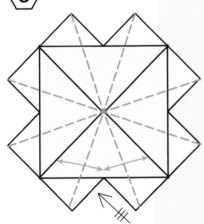

Valley crease corners to centerline.

⟨11⟩

 45°

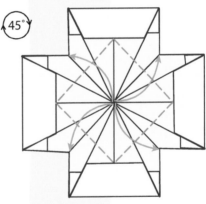

Fold top petals back as desired. Then expand bottom structure to complete the box.

⟨9⟩

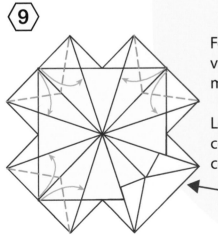

Fold corners to valley crease made in step 8.

Lower right corner shown completed.

⟨10⟩

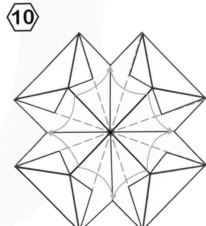

Flop triangular structures along creases made in step 8.

Rinaldi Box

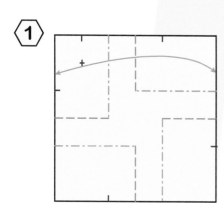

① Mark 1/2 and 1/3, then crease along center to 1/3 mark.

Mountain crease along thirds to crease just made. Turn paper over if necessary.

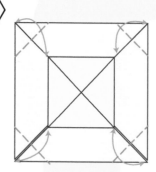

⑥ Form valley crease through all layers on each corner.

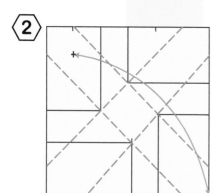

② Valley crease corners to opposite 1/6 landmark to form diagonals.

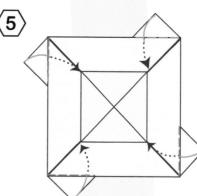

⑤ Valley fold triangular segments under rim, concealing them.

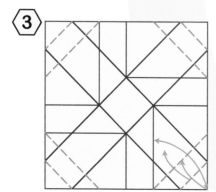

③ Crease corner to near 1/3 mark, then halve and fold a rim.

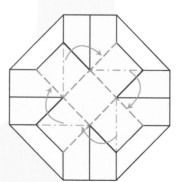

④ Swivel mountain segments over adjacent valleys to create multiple layers shown in step 5.

281

7 Form valley creases through all layers on all four sides.

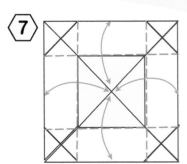

8 Turn model over and valley crease top layer only as shown.

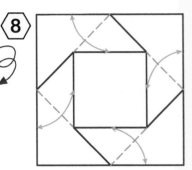

10 Mountain fold the square segments on the outer rim back against the box wall, concealing.

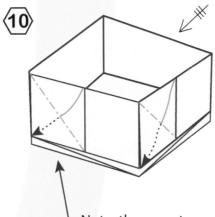

9 Grasp bottom layer only where shown. Pinch and swivel triangular structure beneath the base. Model becomes 3D. Repeat for all sides.

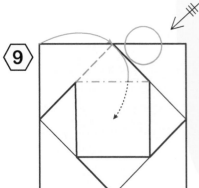

Note: there are two wall structures in each corner. Only swivel lower one in step 9.

Elkwood Box

1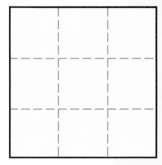

Color side down, crease in thirds.

6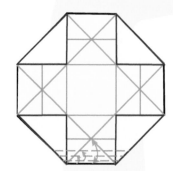

Return corners to 1/3 mark (from step 4). Valley crease edges to 1/6 intersection. Divide that into thirds. Roll edge twice.

2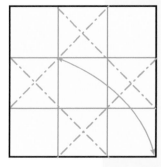

Mountain crease diagonals (Turn over and crease corners to opposite 1/3 intersection).

5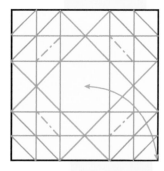

Mountain crease these diagonals. (Turn over and crease corners to center; crease only where shown).

3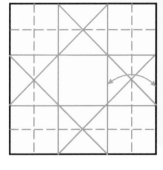

Crease edges to near 1/3 intersection on all four sides.

4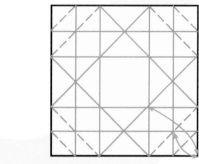

Crease all four corners to near 1/3 intersections then crease corners to diagonal just made.

48

⑦ Repeat step 6 for the remaining sides.

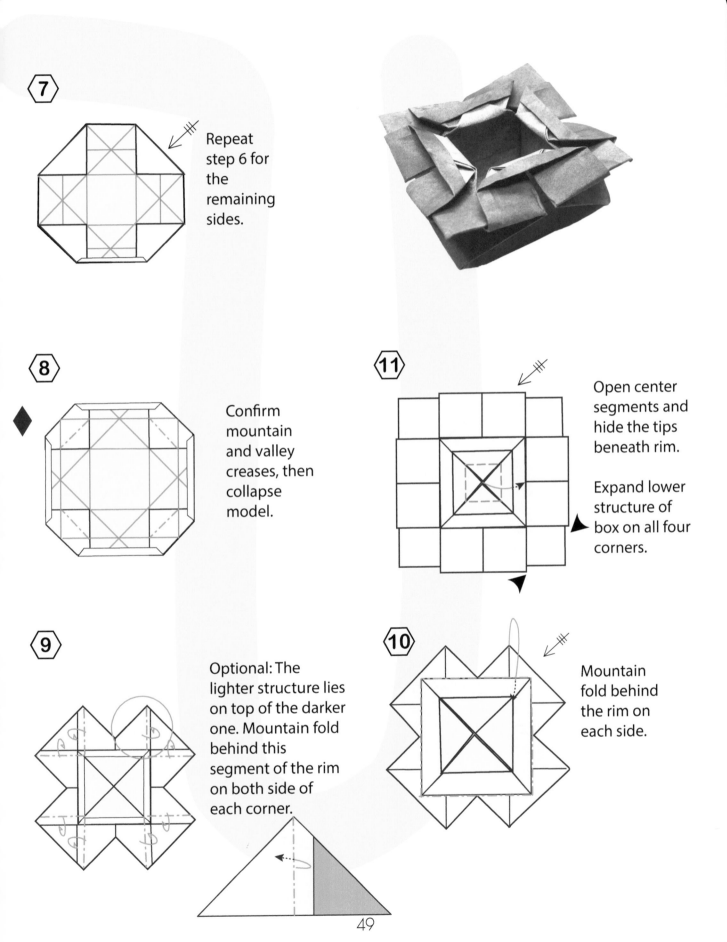

⑧ ◆ Confirm mountain and valley creases, then collapse model.

⑪ Open center segments and hide the tips beneath rim.

Expand lower structure of box on all four corners.

⑨ Optional: The lighter structure lies on top of the darker one. Mountain fold behind this segment of the rim on both side of each corner.

⑩ Mountain fold behind the rim on each side.

Strathern Box

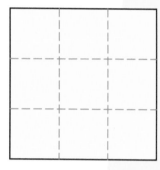

Color side down, crease in thirds.

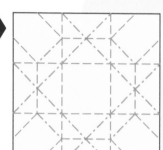

Turn over and collapse model along existing crease lines.

②

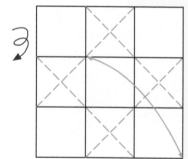

Turn over and crease diagonals.

⑤

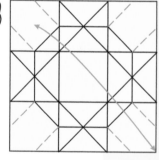

Valley crease diagonals using opposite 1/6 point as landmark.

③

Turn over and crease edge to near 1/3 in center panels only.

④

Turn over and crease diagonals by aligning corners to center point.

299

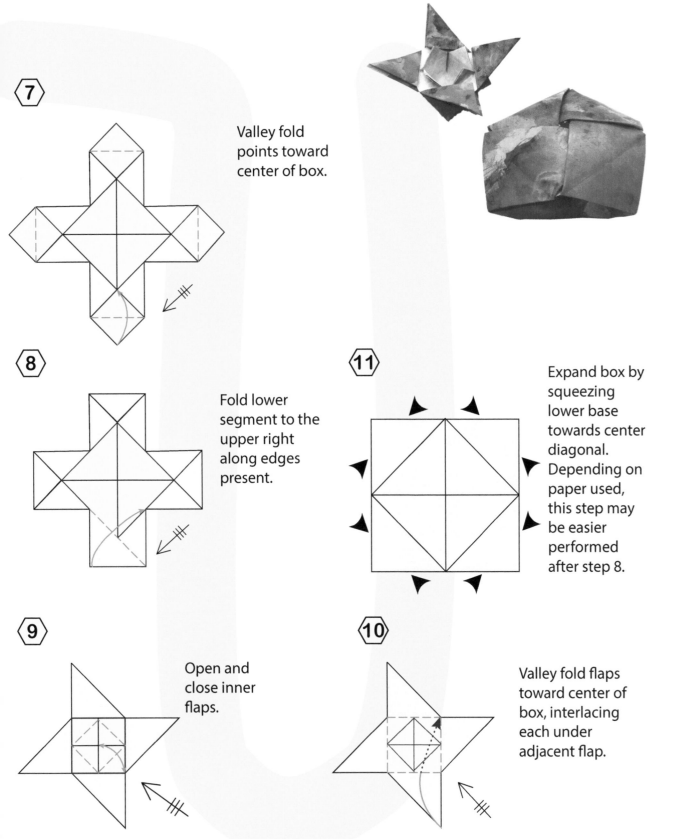

⑦ Valley fold points toward center of box.

⑧ Fold lower segment to the upper right along edges present.

⑪ Expand box by squeezing lower base towards center diagonal. Depending on paper used, this step may be easier performed after step 8.

⑨ Open and close inner flaps.

⑩ Valley fold flaps toward center of box, interlacing each under adjacent flap.

Decorative Option:
To reveal inside color
(shown in photo), from
step 7:

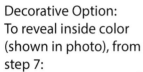 Fold corner
to adjacent
edge.

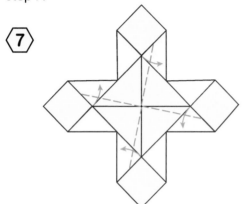

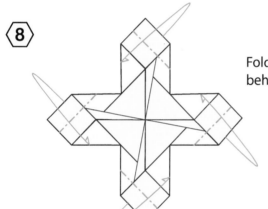 Fold flap
behind.

Close box,
tucking
flaps under
adjacent
flaps.

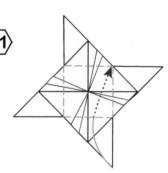

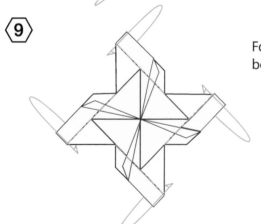 Fold flap
behind.

Tuck
triangle
behind
flap.

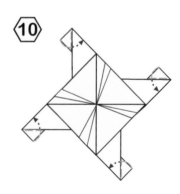

Chatsworth Box

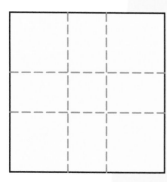

Color side down, crease inner 1/4 (mark 1/2 and 1/4; crease edge to opposite 1/4 mark).

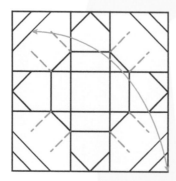

Using opposite 1/8 as a landmark, valley crease diagonals.

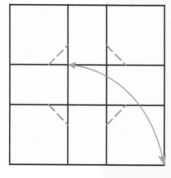

Align corners to opposite intersection and crease only short diagonal shown.

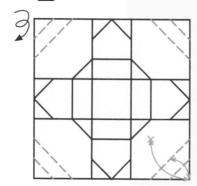

Turn over and valley crease corners to 1/4 mark and then once more to crease just made.

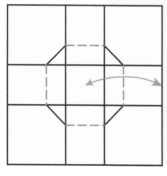

Valley crease edge to center in center panels only.

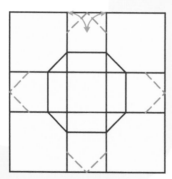

Valley crease center panels at 45 degrees.

 7

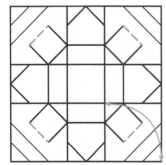

Valley crease diagonals by aligning corner to near 1/3 landmark.

 8

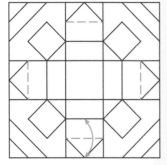

Valley crease edges to near 1/4 mark in center panels.

13

Press on outside as shown to expand box.

12

Fold upper flaps under rim.

11 ◆

Focusing on one outer rim segment at a time, collapse the model along existing crease lines.

These points meet.

9

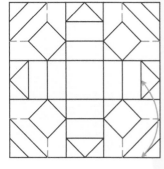

Using the halfway point along outer 1/8, valley crease short segments shown.

10

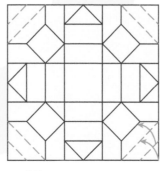

Fold corners to 1/4 diagonal then flop once again for a rim.

Morgana Box

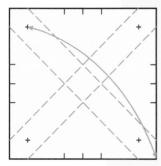

Mark 1/2, inner 1/4 and outer 1/8.

Valley crease corners to opposite 1/8.

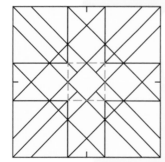

Reverse base to valley creases.

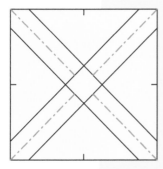

 Mountain crease along inner diagonals.

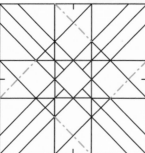

Turn over and reverse diagonals shown to mountain creases.

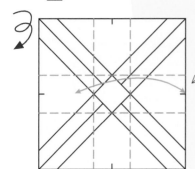

Turn over and valley crease along inner 1/4 (crease edges to opposite 1/4 mark, rotate and repeat).

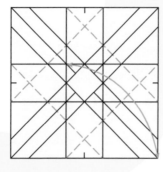

Crease corners to opposite inner 1/4

306

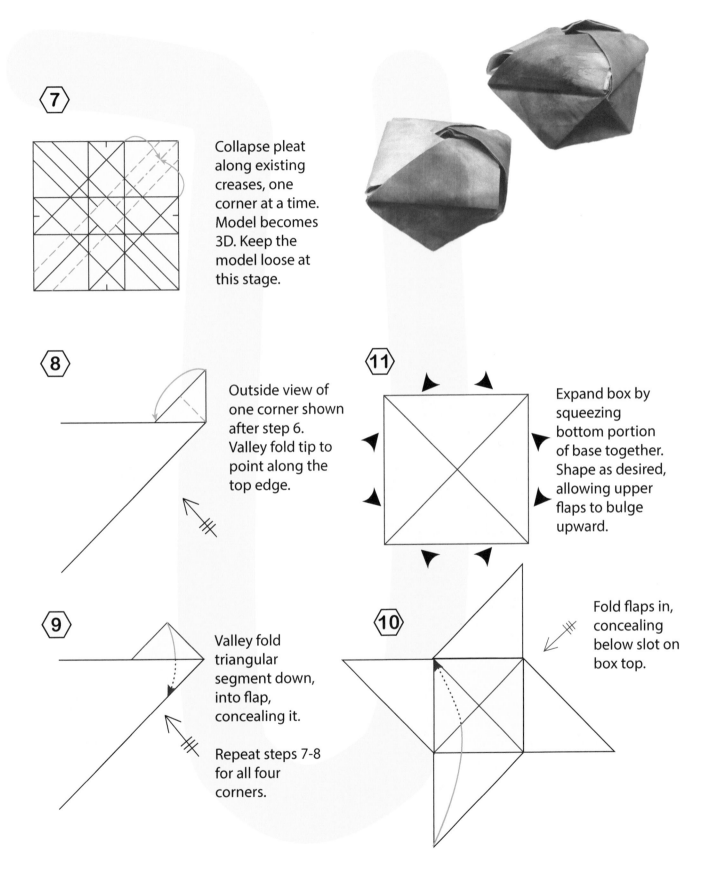

⟨7⟩

Collapse pleat along existing creases, one corner at a time. Model becomes 3D. Keep the model loose at this stage.

⟨8⟩

Outside view of one corner shown after step 6. Valley fold tip to point along the top edge.

⟨9⟩

Valley fold triangular segment down, into flap, concealing it.

Repeat steps 7-8 for all four corners.

⟨11⟩

Expand box by squeezing bottom portion of base together. Shape as desired, allowing upper flaps to bulge upward.

⟨10⟩

Fold flaps in, concealing below slot on box top.

Paper Preparation

I used several types of paper for the models in this book. Gray and tan elephant hide papers were obtained in large format and cut to 9″ squares (Photo 1). My daily use paper for folding is text weight Parchtone from the French Paper company (Photo 2). Both have been dyed using india ink as shown in the following photos. Typical results shown on the next page.

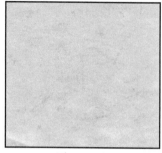

Photo 1

Photo 2

India inks ready.

Paper, sponge and clips.

Inking with sponge.

Drying outdoors.

Clips used while drying.

Without clips, the paper curls

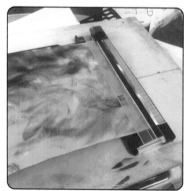

Ready for cutting.

Stacks ready for folding.

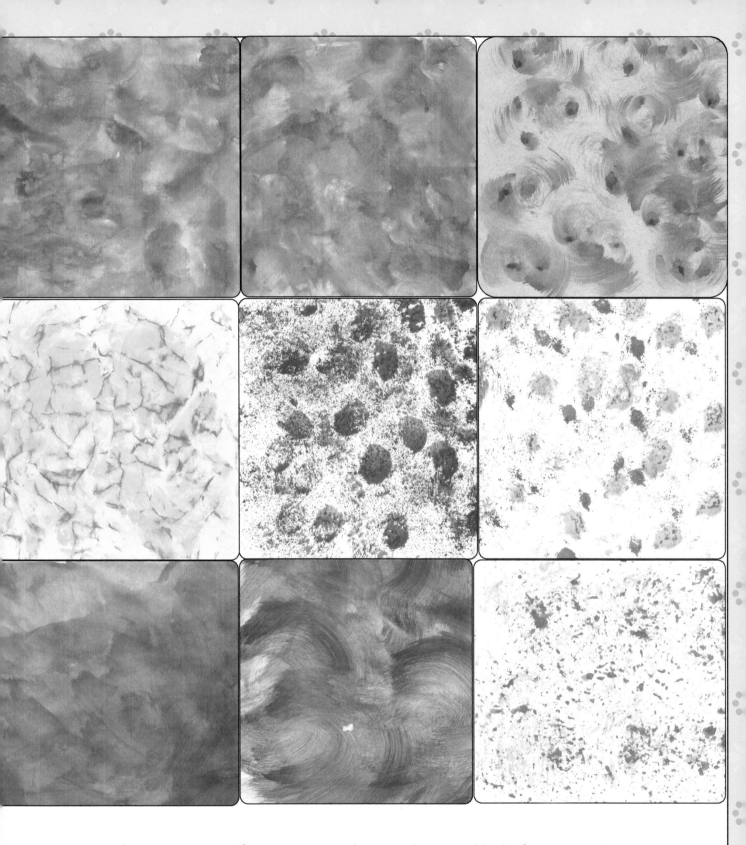

Parchtone is an animal-free imitation parchment with an aged look of papyrus and can be crinkled, inked and then ironed (see middle left example). I often experiment with glues, starches, and coatings for a unique finish.

About the Author

Bradley Tompkins is a cultural creative living in Los Angeles, California and a member of the Pacific Ocean Paperfolders, Origami USA and the international Convention for Creators (CFC). He has been practicing origami and craftwork for over 40 years. Mr. Tompkins holds a bachelor's degree in English Language and Literature and a master's degree in Management Information Systems. As a former online college instructor along with his wife, Bradley has been teaching online and creating curriculum for learners in homeschool, high school, and higher education settings for over 20 years.

Special Thanks

This book was made possible through the steadfast support of my wife, Catherine, who has tolerated bags of boxes and countless hours of my late-night folding and diagramming obsession for over 30 years. Thanks also to Nicole Tompkins, whose excellent photography, design and editing skills are evident throughout the book. Many thanks to Sundy Triantafyllopoulou for folding and diagram proof-reading feedback. Others for whom I am grateful for their encouragement or inspiration: Joel Stern, Arnold Tubis, Nick Robinson, Jerrod Needle and the good people at Origami USA and Pacific Ocean Paperfolders.

Milton Keynes UK
Ingram Content Group UK Ltd.
UKHW021702150724
445684UK00010B/19